Goldfish Care

The Complete Guide to Caring for and Keeping Goldfish as Pet Fish

Tabitha Jones

Tabitha Jones

ISBN: 9781799126553

CONTENTS

INTRODUCTION

Before purchasing any fish it is important to understand that as a fish owner you are responsible for the care and wellbeing of your fish. It is important to try and learn as much as you can about the fish you are considering to keep. You need to make sure that your lifestyle, household and financial status are suited to provide your fish with the best possible care. This guide has been designed to provide you with both precise and concise information about a Goldfish's basic needs to help you provide your fish with the best quality care and aquarium practices. This guide also goes into the benefits of cycling, having a decent filtration system, plants and how to plant them.

DESCRIPTION

The Goldfish (scientifically known as Carassius Auratus) is a freshwater fish in the Cyprinidae family. It is not common knowledge but the goldfish comes from the same family as the Koi Carp and the Curcian Carp! The goldfish is native to east Asia and was first domesticated in China over one thousand years ago! Goldfish breeds vary greatly in body shape, fin shape and configuration, body size and coloration (various combinations of white, red, orange, yellow, brown and black are common). The gold fish is unarguably one of the most popular fish species to be kept in a home aquarium.

Length and Lifespan

Goldish come in a variety of sizes but will commonly grow to around 4 inches (10cm) in length. However it is not uncommon for them to grow to between 7 and 8 inches (18 to 20cm) if they are kept in a spacious tank! Goldfish will commonly live for around 30 years if they are kept in the correct conditions. The oldest living goldfish lived to be over 43 years old!

Goldfish Bowl

Here at Fish Care Manuals we consider keeping a

goldfish in a bowl to be utterly unacceptable and cruel. It is a common misconception that a goldfish can thrive in a small bowl but living in a confined space with no filtration system is severely damaging to their health. Due to the rounded sides the bowl, there is little surface area for oxygen exchange and are generally dramatically too small to house a goldfish.

Vision

Goldfish have one of the most studied senses of vision through all aquatic animals. Goldfish have four cone cells within their eyes which are each sensitive to different colors: red, green, blue and ultraviolet. The ability to distinguish between four primary colors classifies goldfish as tetrachromats!

Cognitive Ability

It is a common misconception that goldfish have extremely short term memory. This misconception is dramatically far from the reality! Goldfish use their supreme vision to distinguish between individual human and may be able to recognize their owners. Domesticated goldfish learn to associate humans with food and will commonly 'beg' for food. Goldfish also have the ability to learn socially and will avoid fish they have had unpleasant encounters with in a community tank. A goldfish has a memory-span of about three months.

Tankmates

Goldfish are peaceful fish and should be kept with fish of a similar size and temperament. They live in waters slightly colder than average and this must be taken into account when choosing Tankmates. We recommend keeping them with the following species in a community tank:

- Loaches
- White Cloud Mountain Minnows
- Rubbernose Plecos
- Rosy Barbs
- Zebra Danios
- Red Cherry Shrimp

FISH KEEPING EQUIPTMENT CHECK LIST

Below is a simple list of the most important things to own if you are planning on keeping fish at home. There are many other things which you can own to help improve the quality of your aquarium but this list is the essentials that are necessary to provide a safe and healthy environment for your fish.

Aquarium

An aquarium of at least 20 gallons is recommend for beginners. However larger aquariums are generally more stable and can obviously accommodate either more fish or larger fish. It is important to purchase a specialized fish aquarium rather than a reptile vivarium. Aquariums are designed to hold the weight of the water and will not crack, or break, under the pressure.

Aquarium Gravel

Gravel is the most common substrate used within aquariums. Gravel is course enough to allow water flow while also being fine enough to encourage the growth of nitrifying bacteria. Coarse sands, glass gravel and Creek Stones are all excellent choices. Avoid limestone and calcium based substrates as they will not promote healthy bacteria growth.

Aquarium Filter

Your aquarium filter should be rated to turn over at least 3 to 5 times the aquariums volume each hour. For small aquariums a Hang-On-Back filter is perfect. We recommend using a tried and tested filter, such as the Marineland Penguin Power Filters, as they are proven to be reliable, easy to use and have a high flow rate.

Replacement Filter

It is important to always have a backup filter in case your main one breaks. If you leave your fish in your tank without a working filtration system for too long it will cause them to have sever health problems.

Heater

A heater is essential for limiting the chance of your fish getting diseases. It also allows for the keeping of tropical fish. There are multiple water heater brands that are reliable and affordable. There should be multiple available in your local pet store or aquarium store.

Water Test Kit

It is very important to have a good quality and reliable water test kit. A good quality kit will allow you to test for cycling before introducing fish into your aquarium. Your water test kit is also the apparatus that alerts you to toxic aquarium conditions which could potentially harm your fish.

Fish Food

Fish should be fed at least twice a day and it is therefore recommended to purchases your fish food in bulk to lower the cost. Better quality fish food will result in your fish having brighter and more colorful scales. We recommend using a mixture of color enhancing flakes, regular pelleted fish food and frozen fish food to create variety.

Aquarium Vacuum

The vacuum is the most important piece of cleaning maintenance. It will clear faces and debris from the substrate of your aquarium. Removal of debris will help to reduce the nitrates in the water and help to make your fish not feel stressed. There are multiple brands available that come in at multiple different price points. We recommend the 'Python No Spill Vacuum' – despite being relatively expensive it is the most efficient, reliable and least likely to spill water onto your carpet out of all the vacuums we have used.

Fish Net

Fish nets are useful for removing dead plant matter, excess food and for moving your fish. They are an essential part of the transportation process as you should never touch live fish with your bare hands.

Aquarium Glass Scrubber

An aquarium glass scrubber is essential to keep your tank clean. It is a fish friendly cleaning product that helps keep your aquarium looking fresh and aesthetically pleasing.

5-gallon Bucket

A 5-gallon bucket is a useful piece of equipment as you can store your fish in it in case of a tank emergency. A large bucket is also essential for transporting fish with spiny fins or fish who have a tendency to bite through fish transportation bags.

Decorations

Decorations are a perfect way to improve the aesthetic of your aquarium while also providing your fish with an interesting area to explore. Common decorations range from real and fake plants to specifically made underwater objects – such as castles and treasure chests. There should be a wide range of aquarium decorations available in your local pet store, aquarium store and online.

AQUARIUM SETUP

Once you have purchased everything on the above checklist it is now time to set up your aquarium. Before setting up your aquarium it is important to place it on a hard flat surface. If the surface is slightly slanted it can cause your fish stress and may end up cracking the aquarium glass due to a buildup in pressure. If you have a large aquarium (anything over 30 gallons) it is recommended to place your tank on either a sturdy cabinet or the floor to make sure that it is safe and secure. It is important to place your aquarium near a power socket as extension cables are not desirable for both safety and aesthetic reasons – water and electricity do NOT mix!

NOTE: There will be a separate section talking about filtration systems as it is a complex process.

Cleaning the Substrate

Once you have chosen the location of your tank it is important to choose and clean your substrate. Most people opt for some form of gravel to line the bottom of their aquariums. It is essential that you wash your substrate before putting it into the tank. To clean your substrate place it into a bucket and spray it with a high powered hose. Once the bucket is filled clean the substrate by vigorously moving your hands through the bucket in a circular motion. After a few minutes remove the dirty water from the bucket while leaving the substrate at the bottom of the bucket. Repeat this process at least four more times or until the water is visibly clearer. Some substrates may leave the water slightly cloudy but this is nothing to worry about as the cloudiness will natural settle in your tank over time. The cleaning process is essential to remove dust, bacteria and any potential parasites that may have found their way into the substrate during the storage process.

Placing the Substrate

Once the substrate is clean it is time to use it to line your aquarium. Gently place the cleaned substrate into the bottom of the tank. It is important to line the tank slowly and gently to avoid cracking the glass. It is recommended to use a small scoop to speed up the process. Once you have lined the aquarium it is important to smooth the substrate into about a half inch flat lining.

Filling the Aquarium with Water

It is recommended to fill your aquarium with a hose pipe – filling an aquarium with buckets is a slow process but is possible if there is not a tap nearby. After the tank is full use a water de-chlorinator. Although there are no fish currently in the tank, chlorine and chloramines can build up over time. It is recommended to purchase a high quality de-chlorinator as you will need to use it after every water change.

Heating and Lighting

It is considered best practice to have two heaters in your aquarium. It is important to purchase heaters that will comfortably fit into your tank and not take up too much of the swimming space. Higher wattage heaters are better due to the fact that they save power and will put less stress on the heating system. Once you have chosen your heaters you should stick them to the glass inside your aquarium. It is important to place your heaters in a place that has a good water flow to help spread the warmer water throughout the tank. You should heat your tank to between 60 and 75 degrees Fahrenheit (15 to 24 degrees Celsius). Most heaters will display an orange light when they are on and working. Lights are normally placed above or behind the tank. It is important to purchases lighting that has a timer. Aquariums should not be directly lit for more than 8 hours a day.

FILTER

The purpose of the filter is to remove excess food, dangerous chemicals, decaying organic matter, feces and any other unwanted floating particles. Fish excrete waste constantly as they swim around in the water. If this waste is not removed quickly and efficiently, the toxins that the fish are excreting will build up to a high concentration which may cause the fish to poison themselves. Filters are also a great way to keep your tank looking clean and to keep the water clear and cloudless. It is vitally important to the health of your fish to provide them with a sufficient filtration system. There are three main types of filtration systems used in aquariums which will be discussed below. It is recommended to have multiple different types of filters within your aquarium as it will provide the best results and will provide a failsafe filtration system if one breaks down or stops functioning as desired.

Biological Filtration

Biological filtration involves bacteria, microorganisms and fungi converting the waste your fish produce into less toxic substances. As previously mentioned your fish excrete waste constantly as they swim and this waste if not removed will become poisonous to your fish. A biological filter will convert the ammonia in the waste into nitrite, and then the nitrite into nitrate. Nitrate is dramatically less harmful than anomia and nitrite. However nitrate does have some harmful side effects such as causing a loss of appetite, eye problems and kidney failures in your fish. Biological filtration is established during the cycling process (there will be an in depth section on cycling following this one). Biological filtration is necessary in every aquarium but should be accompanied with either mechanical or chemical filtration.

Mechanical Filtration

Mechanical filtration is the process of removing physical waste and unwanted particles. Mechanical filtration works by forcing the water to pass through a strainer. The strainer will not allow unwanted particles to pass through it. The most common materials used for strainers are sponge, filter floss, special filter pads and even aquarium gravel. The finer the material used for the strainer the smaller the particles that can be caught. However finer materials will need to be rinsed and replaced more often due to the fact that they will get plugged and dirtied at a faster rate. Many mechanical filters will use a mixture of fine and coarse materials to create their strainers and to provide the optimal balance between water cleaning and filter maintenance. It is important to clean your filter on a regular basis as it will help to optimize the filtration process. Leaving a dirty filter plugged in will prevent sufficient water flow and may even force water to flow around the filter itself.

Chemical Filtration

Chemical filtration is provided by either carbon or chemical resins. The resins extract toxins from the water in a similar way to a biological filter but are much more aggressive and effective. Chemical filters are extremely efficient until they are saturated with toxins – once they are saturated they provide no filtration and will therefore need to be changed as soon as possible. Typically 1 square inch of carbon can provide filtration to 2 gallons of water. It is important that your water flow allows for the entire tanks volume to pass through the carbon filter at least every 2 hours or it will not be sufficiently filtered.

Problems with Chemical Filtration

Chemical filtration has a few problems which makes it not advisable for beginner fish keepers. If you use water that is has a high amount of minerals or chemicals in it this will vastly increase the rate in which your chemical filter becomes saturated. Adding fish food, minerals, trace elements, having an overcrowded tank or having insufficient water changes can also quickly over saturate your filter. If your filter becomes overly saturated, and does not get changed, it can start to release the toxins back into the water which negates its previous filtration.

CYCLING

Cycling is the most important part of setting up your new aquarium. Fish waste and excretions produce ammonia, and as previously mentioned this ammonia is toxic to fish. This ammonia is changed into nitrite and then into fish safe nitrate. Your aquarium is a delicately balanced ecosystem that is dependent on this nitrogen cycle. The process of destroying 'bad' bacteria generates 'good' bacteria that your fish need to survive.

Fishless Cycling

It used to be common to introduce hardy fish into your aquarium during the cycling process. The ammonium found in the fish waste helps to kick start the growth of bacteria and start the cycling process. However it is no longer considered best practice as it is cruel and leads to either health problems or the death of the hardy fish. It is possible to directly add ammonia to the aquarium. Initially 2-4ppm of ammonia should be added into your aquarium, with small amounts being added every few days.

Water change

It is recommended to do a 10-15% water change every day during the cycling process. This will prevent the buildup of ammonia.

Introducing Fish

It is important to leave your new tank for at least one day before introducing any fish to it. It is considered best practice to wait between 2-8 weeks before introducing fish to make sure that the cycling process has fully ended and to minimize the chance of any fish dying. When introducing new fish make sure that the ammonia and nitrite levels do not dramatically spike as this will be harmful to both your old fish and the new ones.

WATER CARE SCHEDULE

It is vital to maintain a healthy environment for your fish. Keeping your water to a high standard is a big commitment. It is possible to keep your aquarium in great shape by following this simple schedule.

Daily

- Check the temperature of the water.
- Look for any issues with the filtration system and to make sure that the water is clear.

Weekly

- Remove 10-15% of the tanks water and replace it with de-chlorinated water.
- Test the water conditions. Make sure that the pH, ammonia, nitrite, nitrate, alkalinity, chlorine level and hardness are normal. It is advised that you use a water kit for this.
- Clean any excessive buildup of algae.

Monthly

- Perform a 25% water change and change the substrate.
- Check that your filtration systems are

working. Change the filter cartridge, replace carbon and rinse the pre filter if needed.

- Scrub your aquarium to remove all the algae that will have built up.
- Remove plastic decorations and clean them.
- Prune any live plants

PLANTS

Adding living plants to your aquarium is a great way to make your tank look more aesthetically pleasing. Living plants also help with balancing out your tanks water chemistry. There are hundreds of different types of plants that you can add to your tank. It is normally a good idea to stick to one type of plant as it allows them to thrive most efficiently. There are three important variables to get right when using living plants in your tank: lighting, nutrients and carbon dioxide.

Lighting

Lighting is arguably the most important factor when it comes to growing and keeping plants. Sunlight is responsible for the growth of plants and it is therefore important to replicate this with a bright fixture. It is recommended to have between 1-2 watts per gallon of lighting. For example if your tank is 30 gallons, you would want between 30 and 60 watts of light.

Nutrients

Aquatic plants require trace elements and vitamins that do not naturally exist in your tank due to the fact that your aquarium is a closed system. There are two ways to supply your plants with the nutrients they need.

Firstly, a nutrient substrate or gravel can be used – these can be purchased from any large pet store or aquarium store. The second way to give your plants nutrients is to add liquid additives. These liquids contain iron, magnesium, potassium and other elements that plants need. It is recommended to use both methods to optimize the trace elements in your tank.

Carbon Dioxide (CO2)

Carbon dioxide is a major factor that affects the growth rate and overall health of plants. On land plants utilize carbon dioxide in the air. Aquatic plants absorb carbon dioxide through the water. The most effective way to provide your aquatic plants with CO2 is with a large CO2 canister, hollow tubing and a glass diffuser. However this set up is very expensive and is therefore not recommended for beginners. A more affordable option is to use a liquid form of carbon, such as 'Flourish Excel' made by Seachem, as it can easily be absorbed by the plants.

The Most Common Plant Types

The follow are among the most common types of plants used in home aquariums:

- Stem Plants

- Anubais and Ferns
- Moss
- Hair Grass
- Potted Plants

There will be a section after this one which explains about the best practice for introducing these five types of plants into your aquarium.

THE PLANTING PROCESS

Planting your aquarium is an important process and you should take some time deciding where you wish to place each plant. It is also important to plan how you expect the plant to grow over the next few months and how it will end up looking. During the planning process you also need to consider where you will place any other decorations (such as interesting rocks, drift wood and plastic aquarium decorations). The following sub-sections will outline the best planting practices for each of the most commonly used plant types.

Stem Plants

Stem plants normally come with a wire around their base which holds the stems together. When planting a stem plant you must first remove this wire and carefully separate each stem. Stem plants can be planted in a large bunch or separated – it depends on what you personally find most appealing. Stem plants quickly grow so do not be worried if they do not completely cover the areas where you plant them. Stem plants also allow for you to propagate them by using the tops of the plants! Due to their large size stem plants are a great way to hide your filter and heating system. To plant you should push the stems about an inch or two into the substrate. It will not take long for stem plants to establish a strong root system.

Anubais and Ferns

Anubais and fern plants will need to be attached to either submerged rocks or wood within your aquarium as this is how they grow in nature. It is considered best practice to wedge these plants between rocks or tie them in place as they have a tendency to become uprooted and float away. If you are choosing to tie your plants in place we recommend using either cotton thread or fishing wire as they will not break or release harmful toxins into the water. Cotton thread is probably a better choice as it does not have the potential to restrict the plants growth.

Moss

Moss should be placed onto the rocks and wood within your aquarium. Moss is a very popular choice for beginner aquatic plant keepers due to its hardy nature and the way it sways in the water. Moss has an increased growth rate the closer it is placed to the surface of the water and it is therefore important to plan where you will place it. You should tie your moss, using cotton thread or fish wire, to the desired area in a similar way to how you tie Anubais plants. It is also possible to plant moss by placing a carbon filter on top of it to secure it in place. By the time the carbon filter because overly saturated the moss should have taken root in the desired location.

Hair Grass

Hair grass is a relatively cheap aquatic plants and is therefore a common choice for people to use in their aquariums. It can thrive in lower light and is relatively hardy which again adds to its popularity. Hair grass grows along the bottom of your aquarium in a similar fashion to grass found on land. When planting hair grass it is important to minimize your handling of its roots as they are very fragile. Plant each stem about half an inch into the substrate and about half an inch away from the others to allow for each stem to properly grow and spread - hair grass will spread natural and densely!

Potted Plants

Potted plants will generally come in small clay, or plastic, pots with cotton thread to protect their root structure. It is important to remove the cotton thread and the plant from its pot before attempting to plant. Once removed from the pot it is considered best practice to dig a small hole in the substrate for your plant's root system. Once in the hole you should carefully cover the roots. It will not take long for the roots to become fixed in place and for your plant to start growing.

TRANSPORTING YOUR FISH

It is inevitable that you will one day have to transport your fish to a new location. You will definitely, at least, have to transport your fish after purchasing them. It is not considered best practice to transport your fish in their aquarium due to the fact that aquariums are heavy and could easily break. It is therefore considered a safer strategy to transfer your fish into smaller containers and empty your aquarium before transportation. The following section will outline the best practices for transporting fish.

Plan your Journey Carefully

It is considered best practice to not transport your fish unless it is absolutely necessary. Fish are not hardy creatures and therefore it requires a high level of planning to transport them safely and successfully. If you are planning on flying to a new location you will need to make sure that your airline will allow you to transport fish. If you contact your airline well in advance of your flight they can advise you on what measures they suggest, and require, for you to take. If you are planning on transporting your fish by car your final destination can be no further than 48 hours away from your start point. If fish are in transit for more than 48 hours their chance of survival decreases dramatically. If your journey requires you to stay at a hotel, or similar accommodation, overnight it is important to make sure that you are allowed to bring your fish with you into the building. You cannot leave your fish in a vehicle overnight as the change in temperature is likely to be fatal. It is important to try to minimize transit time as much as possible.

Things to Consider

It is important to remember that any mistake, even one that seems minor, can have a huge effect on the health of your fish. You should never take your fish with you on short vacations. If you are going on vacation it is considered best practice to find someone to care for your fish in your home (to avoid the risks of transportation). If transportation is completely necessary it is important to make no unnecessary stops. It is important to remember that the longer your fish are in transit the higher the risk that their health will suffer. It is possible to mail your fish. However this process is considered risky as you are depending on there being no delays and no one mishandling your fish. If you have fragile fish and are going to be traveling a long distance it may be worth considering rehoming your fish. You can always purchase new fish but you cannot bring a fish back to life or solve severe health problems caused through the transportation process.

Preparing to move your Fish

It is considered best practice to not feed your fish for between 24 and 48 hours before transporting them. Fish can survive a few days without food but being transported in water that is contaminated with fecal waste could be dangerous to their health. Before removing your fish from the aquarium it is considered best practice to first remove, and bag, the ornaments from your tank. By bagging the ornaments it allows you to preserve the beneficial bacteria that has grown on them.

Bagging your Fish

When bagging your fish you should use bags designed specifically for this purpose – you can purchase them from any pet store or aquarium supply store. Fish bags are designed to be hardy and stretchy. It is important to fill your fish bags 1/3 full with water from your tank as it is full of the bacteria that your fish is used to. If you fill the bag more than 1/3 there will not be enough air in the bag to keep the water oxygenated which will lead to your fish dying. When removing your fish from their tank it is considered best practice to use a specially designed fish net and to avoid touching your fish with your bare hands. Once your fish is inside the bag it is best to fill the bag with as much air as possible. To do this we recommend placing the fish bag about 5 inches below your mouth and blowing down into the bag to encourage air around the bag to enter it. You should NEVER place your mouth inside the opening of the bag as you will be breathing out harmful carbon dioxide. The jostling of the transportation process will adequately mix the air in the bag with the water. You can simply seal your fish bags by using rubber bands – but you have to make sure that they are sealed tightly to make sure that your fish is safe and secure. It is best practice to transport bagged fish in an insulated cooler. The insulation will help to keep the temperature of the water fairly constant during the journey. The darkness of the cooler will also encourage the fish to be less active during the transportation process. It is important to pack your fish bags tightly into the cooler to provide your fish with enough water to swim in. If they are loosely packed there is a chance the bags will fall over which could result in your fish suffocating. If you do not have enough fish bags to fill your cooler we recommend filling the space with something soft such as a towel. If you have fish that have spiny fins, or may bite through a bag, it is considered best practice to place them in a clean plastic bucket that is 1/3 full of water and has a tightly closing lid.

How to return a Fish to the Tank

Before returning your fish to the tank it is important to make sure that the tank is set up correctly. If you are satisfied with the setup of the tank then it is time to introduce your fish to their new home. Take your bagged fish and float the bags in the water until the temperature of the water in the bag is equal to that of the tank. Once the water temperature is even simply empty the bags into the water. If you transported your fish in a bucket it is considered best practice to catch your fish with a net and introduce it directly into the new tank. It is important to not stress your fish after a new move so it is recommended to feed them lightly over the next few days and to not introduce new fish to the tank to allow your current fish to adjust.

COMMON FISH DISEASES

The following section will help you to identify the five most common fish diseases as well as giving you simple tips on how best to treat them. The majority of common fish diseases and illnesses are caused by having poor water quality or there being an imbalance in the water chemistry. Poor water quality leads to the fish becoming stressed which is the main cause of most of their illnesses and diseases. Fish can also be carriers of parasites or bacteria without showing signs of disease. It is therefore important to closely monitor the fish in your aquarium for a few days after introducing new fish.

General Things to Watch For

The following list is the most important things that would suggest that your fish has an illness or a disease:

- Unusual swimming patterns
- Fins appearing to be pinned to the body
- Abdominal swelling
- Inflamed or discolored skin or fins
- Scraping of the body on rocks

White Spots

If your fish develops small white spots on its fins or

body this is a sign for concern. The white spots infection is normally caused by stress. The white spots are produced by a small protozoan disease causing parasite. It is highly contagious and needs to be treated as soon as you notice it. There are many brands of white spot treatments available to purchase from a pet store or an aquarium store so it is recommended to ask in store for advice.

Fin Rot

As the name suggests, fin rot is a disease that is located on the fish's fins. It can be recognized by the fin becoming opaque or looking blood-streaked. Fin rot begins in the tip of a fish's fin and slowly spreads to the base. If the disease is allowed to reach the base of the fish's fin it will most likely end in the death of the fish. Fin rot is normally caused by either poor water quality or from other fish nipping at the fish's fins. Fin rot is treatable and you can easily purchase anti-bacterial medicine to treat the disease from any pet store or aquarium store.

Fungal Infections

There are always spores of fungus present within aquariums to help create good bacteria. However sometimes this fungus can become infectious if a fish already has damaged skin, fins or gills. The main signal that a fish has a fungal infection is a white, cotton like growth on their body. Anti-fungal medicines are available from any pet store or aquarium store.

Cloudy Eyes

This disease affects your fish's eyes and vision. It is easily noticeable due to the fact that your fish's eyes will become cloudy. Parasites in your aquarium are the most common cause of cloudy eyes however old age, stress and malnutrition can also cause this condition. The easiest way to cure the cloudy eye disease is to improve the quality of the water within your tank. Once the water quality within the tank is a good enough quality your fish will normally recover in about 1 to 2 weeks.

Swim Bladder Disease

Swim bladder disease is serious as it directly affects your fish's ability to control its buoyancy. If you notice that a fish spends most of its time either at the top or bottom of the tank it is likely that they are suffering from this disease. Within the fish keeping community there is a huge debate on what causes this disease and how best to treat it. We recommend asking the establishment where you purchased your fish on the best course of action to treat this disease.

FINAL THOUGHTS

Thank you for purchasing our fish care manual on caring for Goldfish. We hope you have found the information both interesting and informative. We hope that this book has allowed you to make an informed choice on whether owning a Goldfish suits you and if so we hope that the information will help you to provide the best quality care for your new fish.

We will be publishing multiple other fish care manuals on our author page on both Amazon and Kindle. If you have an interest in exotic and exciting fish then we highly suggest you check out our other work.

I am passionate about providing the best quality information to our customers. We would highly appreciate any feedback, or reviews, you could leave us on our Amazon page. Your feedback allow us to help create the best possible fish care products available on the market.

Goldfish Care

CObY

Printed in Great Britain
by Amazon